Legend of Damu

R.Kalyana Krishnan

BlueRose ONE.com DIY
Stories Matter
NewDelhi • London

BLUEROSE PUBLISHERS
India | U.K.

For permissions requests or inquiries regarding this publication,
please contact:

BLUEROSE PUBLISHERS
www.BlueRoseONE.com
info@bluerosepublishers.com
+91 8882 898 898
+4407342408967

ISBN: 978-93-7139-286-0

First Edition: June 2025

PREFACE

In the quaint town of Kedarpur lives an ordinary man named Damodar—Damu to those who kn him. He's not particularly strong or brave, nor does he possess any supernatural abilities. In fc what makes Damu special is quite the opposite: his endearing absent-mindedness.

Damu forgets errands, misplaces items, and stumbles through life with a kind heart anc perpetually confused expression. His wife Lakshmi manages their modest home with patience c wisdom, while their spirited daughter Vidya navigates childhood with her father's good nature c her mother's sharp intellect.

But fate has a curious sense of humour, and in Damu's case, it manifests in the most unexpec ways. Through a series of coincidences, missteps, and happy accidents, this unassuming m repeatedly finds himself at the centre of extraordinary circumstances—defusing terrorist plc foiling robbery attempts, and saving lives, all without the slightest intention of doing so.

These eight interconnected tales chronicle the adventures of Kedarpur's most unlikely hero—a m whose forgetfulness becomes his greatest strength, whose stumbles become steps toward just and whose confusion constantly confounds criminals. From accidentally swapping bags wit terrorist to inadvertently pulling a train's emergency chain just before disaster, Dan misadventures have transformed him into a local legend.

As you turn these pages, you'll meet the colourful cast of characters who orbit Damu's world: loyal Inspector Ranjith, whose friendship and quick thinking complement Damu's accider heroics; the strong-willed Lakshmi, whose love for her husband never wavers despite his foib and brave young Vidya, who inherits her father's knack for inadvertent heroism.

In a world that often celebrates planned perfection, these stories remind us that sometimes most remarkable outcomes arise from our most human moments—our mistakes, our accide and our ability to bumble headfirst into exactly the right place at exactly the right time.

Welcome to the world of Damu, where heroism happens by mistake and saving the day is another unexpected outcome of forgetting where you put your keys.

Contents

1. “The Absent-Minded Hero”
2. “The Unintentional Saviour Strikes Again”
3. “The Highway Heroics”
4. "Forgotten Cash, Unforgettable Night”
5. “Damu’s Daughter: Vidya’s Daring Rescue”
6. “Track of Destiny: How Damu Saved the Night”
7. "Damu’s Flask of Justice"
8. “The Misstep that Saved the Bank”

EPISODE - 1

"The Absent-Minded Hero"

In the small, picturesque town of Kedarpur, lived a 45-year-old man named Damodar, fondly known as Damu. Everyone in the town loved Damu for his kindness, generosity, and unassuming nature. However, Damu had a reputation for being absent-minded. He would often get lost in his thoughts, wander aimlessly, or forget even the simplest tasks. His wife, Lakshmi, 40 years old, was his perfect match—brilliant, sharp, and patient. She loved Damu for his pure heart and saw his absent-mindedness as an adorable quirk, always keeping things organized to complement his forgetfulness.

The couple had a Ten-year-old daughter named Vidya. They lived in a modest home passed down through generations. Though the house was small, it was warm, welcoming, and filled with love. Life in Kedarpur was simple, with friendly neighbours and a close-knit community. Every evening, Damu could chat with his friends or tend to their small garden, while Lakshmi managed the house gracefully.

One bright morning, Lakshmi reminded Damu to run a few errands in the bustling town market. "Don't forget, we need vegetables, rice, and a few other essentials," she said, handing him a neatly packed bag. "And make sure to be back before lunch!" Damu nodded, humming happily, and set out on his scooter.

Unknown to Damu, a notorious terrorist was planning a sinister attack that very day. The terrorist had planted a bomb inside a seemingly ordinary black bag and was planning to place it in the crowded market, intending to cause chaos and devastation.

As Damu wandered through the market, he marvelled at the vibrant stalls, the aroma of fresh fruits and spices filling the air. Lost in his own thoughts, he roamed from one vendor to another, placing the groceries into his bag. But being his usual absent-minded self, he set his bag down on a bench for a moment while he admired some handicrafts nearby. Meanwhile, the terrorist, who had also been in the market, hurriedly placed the bomb-laden bag on the same bench just beside Damu's grocery bag and left to prepare for his getaway.

After a while, Damu received a call on his mobile phone and headed toward his scooter carrying the bag containing the bomb, thinking that he was carrying his own grocery bag. As he was about to place the bag on the scooter, he noticed a parked jeep nearby and, thinking it was a more convenient place to attend the call, he walked over. While still on the phone, he absentmindedly placed the terrorist's black bag in the back of the jeep. After finishing the call, Damu returned to his scooter, blissfully unaware of the switch he had just made, and headed home without the grocery bag.

When Lakshmi enquired about the groceries, he cut a sorry figure and told her that he had forgotten it somewhere. He promised her that he would buy the groceries once again the next day.

Meanwhile, the terrorist proceeded towards the jeep expecting the bomb to explode any minute in the market. He jumped into the jeep where Damu had inadvertently left the bomb-laden bag. He attempted to flee the town. However, fate had other plans. The bomb, set on a timer, exploded in the terrorist's vehicle as he drove away, causing a loud blast on the outskirts of town.

The sound of the explosion startled the entire town. Police quickly rushed to the scene, and within minutes, they discovered what had happened. The shattered remains of the terrorist's jeep gave them enough clues to realize that the bomb had detonated inside his vehicle. After scanning the area, they also found CCTV footage from the market, showing Damu's innocent mix-up with the bags.

The police team headed by Inspector Ranjith investigated the incident. They were initially puzzled, but when they pieced the story together, they realized that Damu's absent-mindedness had unwittingly thwarted a major disaster. With all the clues and CCTV footage, they were able to trace the terrorists' hideout. They immediately headed to Damu's house, where they found him enjoying tea with Lakshmi, completely unaware of the chaos he had just prevented.

Ranjith explained everything to Damu and Lakshmi, and the news quickly spread across town. The town's quiet hero, Damu, had become a legend overnight. The townsfolk were stunned but thrilled at the unexpected turn of events.

Although Damu had done nothing on purpose, his actions saved countless lives that day. The police commended him, and the town celebrated his newfound status. Damu, in his usual humble way, laughed off the accolades, still somewhat confused about how his absent-mindedness could have led to such a dramatic event.

Lakshmi, beaming with pride, stood by her husband's side as the town honoured him. With the reward money that the police presented to him, Damu and Lakshmi decided to renovate their home, turning it into a beautiful and warm space that welcomed all who visited.

In the months that followed, Damu became a town icon. His innocent charm and good nature endeared him to the people even more. Everywhere he went, people greeted him with admiration and respect. He was often asked to lead community events, help with town projects, and even advise the local school children.

Despite all the attention, Damu remained the same humble, absent-minded man he had always been. He continued his daily routine of running errands and forgetting small tasks, but now with a legendary story to his name. Lakshmi, ever the loving and supportive wife, was there to guide him as always.

Damu's story became a timeless tale in the town, passed down through generations. It was a reminder to everyone that even the most ordinary individuals, with all their quirks and flaws, could perform extraordinary feats of heroism.

EPISODE - 2

"The Unintentional Saviour Strikes Again"

One Sunday evening, Damu, his wife Lakshmi, and their daughter Vidya decided to enjoy the excitement of the annual exhibition in the bustling town of Kedarpur. The exhibition was one of the most anticipated events of the year, drawing crowds from all over the region. Bright lights decorated the venue, casting a festive glow on every corner. Various stalls lined the grounds, offering everything from local delicacies to handmade crafts and traditional toys. Rides towered over the crowds, laughter and music filled the air, and the buzz of chatter made the atmosphere vibrant and lively.

As the family strolled around, Damu marvelled at the array of attractions. Vidya's eyes sparkled with excitement as she dragged her parents from one stall to another, eager to see everything. Lakshmi joined in with equal enthusiasm, enjoying the rare outing together as a family. Amid all the fun, Vidya's voice piped up, "Papa, I'm thirsty. Can we get some water?"

Damu, ever the doting father, looked around for a water stall but found none in sight. In his search, he spotted a restricted area near a temporary police post, marked off with tape and guarded by a few policemen who were observing the crowd. Behind the enclosure, several devices and equipment were set up on tables—some of which Damu mistook for water dispensers. Not wanting to bother the busy police officers, he decided to take a quick look inside, hoping to find something to quench Vidya's thirst.

Stepping closer, he noticed a peculiar-looking button near the front of one of the devices. Curiosity got the better of him, and without realizing what it was, Damu pressed it. Almost immediately, an ear-piercing alarm blared through the exhibition grounds. Bright red lights began flashing, and the words "FIRE ALERT" were displayed on screens at multiple points around the grounds.

Chaos erupted. The visitors, around 350 people, panicked, surging towards the exit gates in a desperate bid to escape what they assumed was a blazing fire. Stalls were abandoned, rides halted, and the once-lively grounds became nearly deserted within moments.

Back near the alarm, the personnel guarding the area rushed over, alarmed by the blaring siren. They found Damu still standing near the button, staring in shock and confusion. When they questioned him, he could only stammer, "I was just looking for some water... I didn't mean to press anything..."

The officials exchanged frustrated glances, realising they now had a security situation on their hands. Not fully convinced by Damu's explanation, they escorted him to the temporary police post for questioning. Meanwhile, across the grounds, the owners of various stalls grew agitated, furious over the sudden alarm that had disrupted their businesses and frightened their customers away.

Inside the police post, Damu's anxiety grew as he waited to explain himself to the authorities. Lakshmi and Vidya, both worried, stood outside, awaiting any news. Just as the police officers were about to begin their questioning, an ear-splitting crash echoed across the grounds. A massive commotion broke out as people ran towards the center of the exhibition grounds, yelling for help.

As the police and Damu's family stepped out to see what was happening, they saw a heart-stopping sight: the giant Ferris wheel, one of the main attractions of the exhibition, had collapsed. The enormous metal structure lay sprawled across the ground, twisted and broken. The seats, thankfully empty after the evacuation, were crushed beneath the wheel's massive weight. Had it been occupied, the consequences would have been catastrophic.

In the chaos, a few loose wires from the Ferris wheel snapped, sparking and igniting a small fire that quickly spread to nearby stalls. The flames climbed high, fueled by the flammable materials used in the temporary structures, and thick, black smoke billowed into the sky.

Fortunately, thanks to the alarm Damu had unintentionally set off earlier, the fire engines were already on standby. The fire personnel, who had initially rushed over to investigate the alarm, now sprang into action. With practiced efficiency, they quickly deployed hoses, aiming powerful jets of water at the flames that had begun to consume the stalls. Their swift intervention prevented the fire from spreading further, and within minutes, the blaze was under control.

Inspector Ranjith, who had arrived to handle the situation, reviewed the scene with a grim expression. As he surveyed the smouldering remains of the Ferris wheel and the burned stalls, he realized the full extent of what could have happened. Had Damu not accidentally triggered the alarm, the exhibition grounds would have been filled with visitors, many of whom would have been in grave danger.

Ranjith turned to Damu, who was standing by with a look of remorse and confusion, still worried he might be held responsible. But instead of reprimanding him, Ranjith placed a hand on his shoulder. "Damu, do you understand what happened here? That alarm you triggered—it cleared the entire area just in time. Without it, we would have faced a disaster. You may have pressed the button by accident, but you saved lives."

Damu blinked, still trying to process the gravity of the situation. He hadn't intended to do anything heroic; he'd simply been looking for water. But fate had turned his innocent mistake into an act of heroism. Overwhelmed with relief and gratitude, Damu thanked Inspector Ranjith, who reassured him that he had done great service to Kedarpur.

The next morning, news of the incident dominated the headlines. Reporters praised the "Unintentional Savior" who had averted a tragedy with his "unorthodox bravery." Damu's photograph, along with his story, was splashed across newspapers and social media, as people celebrated his role in averting what could have been a devastating accident.

Lakshmi and Vidya were beaming with pride as neighbours, friends, and even strangers stopped by their homes to congratulate Damu. Vidya, thrilled by the newfound fame her father had earned, recounted the story to anyone who would listen, adding her own dramatic flair. “My Papa saved hundreds of people!” she declared with a proud smile, her admiration for him shining brightly.

Even the exhibition authorities, initially frustrated by the alarm mishap, extended their gratitude to Damu. They recognized the role he had played, however unintended, in averting a catastrophe, and invited him to an appreciation event, where he received a small award for his “contribution to public safety.”

Days passed, but the impact of Damu’s actions lingered. In Kedarpur, he was fondly referred to as the “Unintentional Savior,” a title he humbly accepted, though he often chuckled at its irony. Friends and family continued to marvel at how a simple act of curiosity had set off a chain reaction, ultimately turning an ordinary man into an extraordinary hero.

Through it all, Damu’s heart remained unchanged. He continued with his daily life, finding joy in his family, his friends, and the little things that brought happiness. But deep down, he held a newfound appreciation for life’s unpredictable twists, the moments where a simple mistake could lead to a profound impact.

In the end, Damu’s story became a beloved tale in Kedarpur, a reminder that sometimes, even the smallest actions can have far-reaching effects. His story of accidental heroism was retold each year, becoming part of the town’s local lore—a testament to the quiet strength and courage that resides in the most unexpected places.

EPISODE - 3

"The Highway Heroics"

Damu, his wife Lakshmi, and their daughter Vidya were eagerly preparing for a journey to Lakshmi's parents' house to celebrate the Pongal festival. It had been a while since they visited, and they were all looking forward to the celebrations, reconnecting with family, and enjoying the special festival dishes that only Lakshmi's mother could make to perfection. Vidya, especially, was thrilled to meet her cousins and spend time at her grandparents' spacious ancestral home.

As the family prepared to leave, Damu dialled the number of his close friend, Inspector Ranjith. He wanted to let him know about their travel plans, just in case. Ranjith, a dedicated officer, was often busy with work, so Damu was not surprised when the call didn't go through. Not thinking much of it, Damu shrugged and put his phone back in his pocket. He knew Ranjith was a man who would always be there in times of need, and little did Damu know, this journey would indeed bring unexpected challenges.

Around 6 p.m., the three boarded the bus to embark on their long journey. The bus was filled with families, solo travelers, and elderly couples—each of them engrossed in their own conversations or enjoying the sights as they prepared for the overnight trip. Soon, they stopped at the well-known Sharma Dhaba for dinner, a popular food spot along the route. Here, passengers eagerly filed out to grab a meal, stretching their legs and sharing laughter over the hearty dishes being served. Damu, Lakshmi, and Vidya enjoyed their dinner and chatted about the excitement awaiting them.

After their meal, the passengers reboarded, and the bus set off into the night. The sound of the engine humming mixed with the low conversations and occasional bursts of laughter from the passengers. About twenty minutes into the ride, Damu's phone rang; it was Ranjith. Damu answered, and the two friends exchanged pleasantries. He mentioned their stop at Sharma Dhaba, unaware that the line would remain connected as he slipped his phone into the pouch on the seat in front of him.

Suddenly, the bus lurched to an abrupt stop. Startled, the passengers looked around, confused. Before anyone could make sense of what was happening, two masked men burst onto the bus, one brandishing a gun and the other a knife. The atmosphere shifted from calm to chaos in a matter of seconds, as terror swept through the bus. The hijackers, intent on looting the passengers, demanded everyone hand over their valuables and mobile phones.

Damu instinctively reached for his phone, intending to hand it over, but Lakshmi quickly nudged him, whispering for him to keep quiet and let the robbers assume he had no valuables. She pretended to search their bags, murmuring to Damu to avoid drawing attention to himself. Damu, taken by her quick thinking, remained silent, although he was unsure of what to do next.

Meanwhile, the line to Ranjith was still open, and as he listened, he noticed the sudden silence from Damu's end. Concerned, Ranjith called out Damu's name over the line, but there was no response. Then he began to hear faint voices that were unfamiliar. It didn't take long for Ranjith to understand that something was wrong. As a police officer, his intuition was sharp, and he quickly recognized the danger in the background noises he overheard. Ranjith immediately alerted the control room and called the highway patrol, instructing them to proceed quickly to the nearest location, which was close to Sharma Dhaba.

Back on the bus, the masked men continued to collect phones, jewellery, and cash from the passengers. When they reached Damu's seat, one of the robbers pointed the knife towards him. Damu froze, fearing the robber might become aggressive. Lakshmi remained composed, calmly explaining that they hadn't brought much cash and that they had left their valuables at home due to the festival expenses. Her calm demeanour seemed to distract the robbers, who then moved on to collect from other passengers.

As they made their way to the back of the bus, the robber with the gun held it pointed toward the passengers, intimidating them into silence. Vidya, who was clutching her small toy, accidentally dropped her hairband. Concerned for her, Damu reached down to retrieve it, just as the armed hijacker was stepping back towards their seat. In a swift, unexpected motion, Damu's movement caused him to trip, and the gun slipped out of the robber's hand, skidding down the aisle.

At that moment, two passengers—a young man and a middle-aged gentleman sitting nearby—sprang into action. The young man tackled the robber, pinning him to the ground, while the middle-aged man grabbed hold of the gun. The other robber, shocked by the sudden turn of events, was momentarily distracted. Passengers in the front rows seized the opportunity to overpower him, wrestling the knife from his grip.

The situation took a swift and dramatic turn as the passengers, now emboldened by the unintentional bravery of Damu and his family, joined forces to subdue both hijackers. It wasn't long before the sound of sirens echoed in the distance—the highway patrol, alerted by Ranjith's call, had arrived on the scene. They swiftly boarded the bus, handcuffing the hijackers and escorting them to the nearest police station.

Once the chaos settled, a wave of relief washed over everyone. Passengers began sharing their accounts of what had transpired, some still visibly shaken, others overwhelmed with gratitude. They unanimously agreed that Damu's accidental trip had been the pivotal moment that disrupted the hijackers' control over the bus.

Meanwhile, Ranjith, who had been coordinating with the highway patrol, called Lakshmi on her phone. He revealed that he had been listening to the entire situation through the live call left on Damu's phone in the seat pouch. It was a serendipitous chain of events that had allowed him to send timely help. Lakshmi couldn't help but laugh at the irony of the situation—what had started as a casual call had ultimately helped save the entire bus.

Upon their arrival at his father-in-law's house, Damu and his family were received like heroes. News of the incident had already reached them, and the relatives were in awe of Damu's unexpected heroism. Though Damu felt his actions were more accidental than intentional, the family celebrated his courage and calm under pressure.

As they settled into the Pongal celebrations, the events of that night took on a greater meaning. Damu had not only safeguarded his family but also protected the lives of every passenger on that bus. His actions, though unplanned, had saved countless people from harm, making the Pongal festival a truly joyous occasion for everyone.

In the days that followed, the story of "The Highway Heroics" spread across the town. Damu became an unlikely hero, admired for his unintentional bravery. Friends, neighbours, and even strangers commended his courage, and Inspector Ranjith praised his friend's quick instincts and humble nature. People often referred to Damu as the "Unintentional Savior," a title he accepted with modesty and a smile.

As the celebrations wound down, Damu reflected on the journey and the unexpected series of events that had unfolded. He was grateful for the safety of his family, the support of the passengers, and the timely intervention of his friend Ranjith. The experience had strengthened his resolve and reminded him of the power of unity and resilience.

For years to come, tales of Damu's heroics on that bus would be recounted in Kedarpur, inspiring others to face challenges with courage and faith

EPISODE - 4

"Forgotten Cash, Unforgettable Night"

It was a busy Saturday morning when Lakshmi reminded her husband, Damu, to draw Rs. 5000 from the ATM after he was done with grocery shopping. Damu, absentminded as ever, nodded as he grabbed his wallet and left the house. After a few hours of haggling at the vegetable market, picking up groceries, and chatting with neighbours, Damu returned home around 9 PM, tired but satisfied with his purchases.

As soon as he stepped into the house, Lakshmi greeted him, quickly scanning the groceries and vegetables. She then asked, "Did you get the Rs. 5000 I asked for?" Damu froze for a moment, scratching his head. "Oh no... I forgot! I'll go right now and withdraw it," he said sheepishly.

Lakshmi sighed, but knowing the money was needed for an urgent payment the next morning, she urged him to go quickly. Damu, tired as he was, had no choice. He grabbed the scooter keys and set off once again into the cool night air, heading toward the town to the nearest ATM.

The roads were quiet, and the occasional streetlamp flickered, casting long shadows. Damu finally arrived at the ATM around 9:30 PM and noticed something strange a van was parked right outside the ATM, looking like one of those vans used to transport currency for refilling ATMs.

Curious, Damu parked his scooter a short distance away and noticed the security guard sitting by the entrance, dozing off with a wooden stick in his hand. His posture seemed unusual, but Damu assumed the guard was simply tired from his long shift. He then spotted two figures inside the ATM booth.

"Must be loading the cash," Damu thought, deciding that it might take a while for the ATM to be ready for public use again. With the urgent need for money still pressing on his mind, he decided to head to another ATM a little further down the road.

By the time he found another ATM and successfully withdrew the Rs. 5000, it was already past 10 PM. The long day was catching up to him, and he felt drained. Wanting a quick break, he stopped at a small roadside parlour for a cold drink. As he sipped on his soda, his mind wandered back to the first ATM, and a strange thought gnawed at him.

"Why was the security guard dozing when the van was there? And where was the driver? Shouldn't someone be in the van?" The questions started piling up, and a sense of unease crept in. Just as Damu was lost in thought, a familiar hand clapped his shoulder from behind. Startled, he turned around to see Inspector Ranjith, his old friend.

"Damu! What are you doing out here so late?" Ranjith asked with a curious smile.

Damu, happy to see him, greeted him back. "Ah, Ranjith! I came to withdraw some money. Actually... something odd happened earlier," he began explaining the events at the first ATM, how the guard was sleeping, and there was no driver in the van.

Ranjith's expression turned serious immediately. "Are you sure about that?" he asked. Damu nodded, describing the scene in more detail.

Without wasting another moment, Ranjith pulled out his phone and contacted the local patrol unit. "We might have a situation here. Meet me near the ATM on West Street, right by the old bakery. I'll be there shortly." He then turned to Damu, "Come with me. We need to check this out."

Damu, feeling a sense of responsibility, agreed, and the two jumped into Ranjith's police jeep, speeding toward the ATM. As they neared the spot, the patrol team arrived too, and together they approached the scene cautiously.

The van was still there. The security guard was still in his chair, but this time it was clear—he wasn't just sleeping. He was unconscious. Ranjith rushed to check the guard's pulse. "He's been drugged!" Ranjith concluded, immediately alerting his team.

Damu and the officers quickly surrounded the ATM, making sure no one could leave unnoticed. They called the bank manager to the scene for further assistance.

As they entered the ATM room, the scene inside was not what Damu had initially thought. Two masked men were hard at work, using gas cutters to break open the ATM's vault. They had sprayed the security cameras with black paint, making them blind to what was happening inside. The masked men, not realizing they were surrounded, continued their efforts to loot the machine.

One of the men heard the footsteps outside and motioned to his partner to hurry up. As they attempted to flee, they were stopped in their tracks by the quick reflexes of Ranjith and his team. A chase ensued, but with the police already surrounding the area, escape was impossible. Both men were arrested on the spot.

The bank manager arrived soon after, thankful that the police had intervened before any major damage had been done. The looters had managed to disable the ATM security features, but thanks to Damu's timely tip, they were caught red-handed before they could get away with the cash.

As Ranjith secured the scene, he turned to Damu and smiled. "Once again, your intuition has saved the day! You have a knack for being in the right place at the right time."

Damu chuckled, rubbing the back of his neck. "I was just looking to withdraw some money! Who knew this would happen?"

The next day, the news of Damu's late-night adventure spread throughout the town. Once again, Damu had become a hero, not through any deliberate act of bravery, but simply by noticing something strange and acting on it.

The bank awarded Damu for his alertness, and the local police commended his efforts. Lakshmi, of course, was proud of her husband, although she couldn't help but laugh at how it all started with him forgetting to withdraw money earlier in the evening.

And so, Damu's reputation as the town's unintentional hero grew even stronger. Wherever Damu went, people were reminded that sometimes, it's the simplest actions that can have the most profound impact.

EPISODE - 5

“The Damu’s Daughter: Vidya’s Daring Rescue”

The day began just like any other in the modest home of Damu, Lakshmi, and their daughter, Vidya. As the sun rose over Kedarpur, Damu sat at the dining table, engrossed in his newspaper, while Lakshmi was busy in the kitchen preparing breakfast. Vidya, their bright seven-year-old daughter, hurried about, getting dressed for school.

"Damu, please set aside that newspaper and help Vidya get ready. It's almost time to leave!" Lakshmi called out from the kitchen, a mix of affection and urgency in her voice. Damu, ever the absent-minded husband, looked up, slightly disoriented, and quickly complied, helping Vidya put on her shoes. After a quick breakfast, Lakshmi reminded Damu to drop Vidya off at school before heading to the market.

With his scooter idling at the gate, Damu packed Vidya's school bag and lunch box bag into the front basket. He absentmindedly placed his mobile phone on top of Vidya's lunch box bag, completely forgetting it as they set off for school. After dropping Vidya off and bidding her a hasty goodbye, he sped away, still unaware that he had left his phone in the basket.

As the school day went on, Vidya discovered her father's mobile phone nestled between her lunch items. Vidya shrugged, put the mobile back into her bag, and continued with her day.

Unbeknownst to Damu, a sinister event was unfolding. A notorious gang of kidnappers had targeted Vidya's school, with plans to abduct several young girls for ransom. Their van was parked just outside the school gates, waiting for the perfect moment to strike. That morning, Damu had made an unplanned stop to refuel his scooter, a delay that, by sheer coincidence, synchronized with the kidnappers' plan.

By afternoon, the gang had made their move. Vidya, along with five other girls, was swiftly taken in a van, their innocent voices muffled as the vehicle sped away. The kidnappers had meticulously timed their operation, thinking they had outsmarted everyone.

When Damu arrived at the school to pick up Vidya, he was puzzled to find her missing. He asked her friends and teachers, but no one had seen her leaving. Panic set in. He rushed to a public phone booth and frantically called Lakshmi, who hadn't heard anything either. Worried and now in a state of desperation, he contacted Inspector Ranjith, recounting everything. The Inspector, recalling Damu's previous "heroic" incident, took the matter seriously and asked him to come to the station immediately.

At the police station, the atmosphere was tense. Lakshmi, shaken and anxious, had already arrived. As they discussed Vidya's disappearance, Lakshmi suddenly remembered Damu's phone being with Vidya. She mentioned it to Ranjith, whose eyes lit up. He immediately called the GPS tracking unit to locate the phone, while sending out alerts across nearby towns. Time was running out.

Meanwhile, Vidya, ever resourceful like her mother, had a plan. The kidnappers had locked the girls in a small room in an abandoned building on the outskirts of Kedarpur. Most of the girls were terrified, but Vidya remained calm. She spotted an attached bathroom with a small window. Realizing it was their only chance, she reassured the other girls and devised a daring escape.

"I'll squeeze out through the window and find help," Vidya whispered. "If anyone comes in, tell them I'm in the washroom." With determination in her eyes, Vidya climbed onto the bathroom commode and managed to slide open the window. The narrow opening barely fit her, but after some effort, she wiggled through and dropped down to the ground outside.

She sprinted across the overgrown yard, her heart pounding, and made it to the nearby highway. By sheer luck, a lorry driver, noticing the frantic child, pulled over. Vidya explained the situation, and the driver, without hesitation, agreed to take her to the police station.

Back at the station, Damu and Lakshmi were discussing their next steps with Ranjith when Vidya walked in, out of breath but unharmed. The room fell silent. Lakshmi let out a cry of relief, rushing to embrace her daughter, while Damu stood frozen, a mix of disbelief and joy washing over him. After a tearful reunion, Vidya recounted the entire ordeal, impressing everyone with her quick thinking and bravery.

With Vidya's directions and the GPS signal from Damu's phone, Ranjith and his team swiftly moved into action. They pinpointed the kidnappers' hideout and organized a rescue mission. Vidya, still clutching her father's hand, accompanied the team as they rushed to the outskirts of Kedarpur. The police surrounded the building, their weapons drawn, and after a tense standoff, they apprehended the kidnappers without incident. The other girls were freed, unharmed, thanks to Vidya's bravery.

The parents of the kidnapped girls were in tears of relief when they learned that their daughters had been rescued unharmed. They gathered at the police station, where they showered Vidya with praise and gratitude. Her quick thinking and courage had thwarted what could have been a tragedy. One by one, the parents approached Damu and Lakshmi, offering their heartfelt thanks.

"Your daughter is a true hero," said one mother, wiping away tears. "We can't thank her enough."

The entire town soon learned of Vidya's bravery, and the family found themselves at the centre of a whirlwind of attention. Damu, who was still processing the events, could hardly believe that his absent-minded ways had somehow led to yet another extraordinary event.

The news of the daring rescue spread quickly through Kedarpur, and the community rallied around the families of the kidnapped girls. The town's relief was palpable, and they decided to organize a small celebration in Vidya's honor. Though the kidnapping had shaken the entire town, Vidya's bravery had restored a sense of security and pride in their close-knit community.

At the town square, a gathering was held where the families of the rescued girls shared their stories and thanked the police, as well as Damu's family. Vidya, still shy from all the attention, stood beside her parents as the townspeople cheered for her.

Lakshmi, who had always been the strong anchor of the family, couldn't hold back her tears. She beamed with pride as people came forward to congratulate them. Damu, too, was overwhelmed by the support and admiration their family received. For a man who was often teased for his forgetfulness, Damu had now become known as the father of a hero.

Damu, ever the humble man, shook his head in amazement at his daughter's courage. As he held her close, he realized that, despite his own flaws and forgetfulness, the real strength of his family lay in the quiet resilience and brilliance of both Lakshmi and Vidya. Together, they were unstoppable.

As the evening drew to a close, the town's folk shared a meal together, each family thankful for their safety. Vidya's act of bravery became a cherished tale in Kedarpur, one that would be told and retold for generations.

The story of Vidya's daring rescue, much like Damu's earlier adventure, became a part of Kedarpur's folklore. The family, modest and content, continued their quiet life, with an even deeper bond now forged through their shared experiences.

And so, the town of Kedarpur had not one, but two unlikely heroes, whose ordinary lives were sprinkled with extraordinary acts of courage.

EPISODE - 6

"Track of Destiny"

Damu, his wife Lakshmi, and their daughter Vidya were buzzing with excitement. It had been a while since they visited Lakshmi's father in Lucknow, and this trip promised joy, family reunions, and a much-needed break from the routine in Kedarpur. After a bus journey to Dehradun, they finally arrived at the railway station, where the crisp evening air greeted them, carrying with it a sense of adventure and the scent of freshly brewed chai from the nearby stalls. Their train, scheduled to depart at 6:30 p.m., stood waiting at the platform, and the family quickly boarded, settling into their two-tier AC compartment.

The cool, dimly lit coach offered a comfortable respite from their travels. By 8 p.m., Damu and his family had their dinner of homemade rotis and sabzi, lovingly prepared by Lakshmi. Vidya, seated next to her mother on the lower berth, chattered excitedly about all the things she planned to do at her grandfather's house. Once dinner was over, they began to prepare for the night. Damu carefully arranged their luggage, placing their heaviest bag on the small shelf near the emergency alarm chain above his upper berth. To prevent it from falling during the train's jerky movements, he even tied the handle of the alarm chain to the bag for added security, not realizing that this simple act would soon set in motion a series of fateful events.

As the train gradually picked up speed, the rhythmic clatter of the wheels became a lullaby, soothing everyone into sleep. Vidya was the first to doze off, her head resting on Lakshmi's shoulder, while Lakshmi closed her eyes, feeling a sense of calm wash over her. Damu climbed up to his berth, yawning as he adjusted the pillow under his head, oblivious to the drama about to unfold.

Unbeknownst to Damu, the weight of their heavy bag was slowly pulling on the emergency alarm chain. Each jolt of the train caused the bag to shift slightly, drawing the chain tighter. Finally, after a particularly sharp lurch, the bag tugged on the chain with enough force to trigger the alarm.

The piercing sound of the emergency brakes cut through the night, jolting everyone awake. Passengers sat up, startled, looking around in confusion as the train came to an abrupt halt, sending whispers of concern rippling through the compartment. The train halted at an unscheduled station. Lakshmi clutched Vidya protectively, her heart racing as she tried to make sense of what was happening.

Within moments, the train guard, accompanied by two Railway Protection Force (RPF) personnel, entered the compartment where Damu and his family were reserved. They traced the source of the alarm to Damu's berth, where they found the luggage hanging awkwardly from the alarm chain. Damu, groggy and disoriented, was quickly woken up by the guard, who was visibly irritated by the disruption.

Realizing what had happened, Damu began to apologize profusely, explaining that he had no intention of pulling the alarm chain. "I just wanted to make sure our bag didn't fall," he said, embarrassed by the commotion he had inadvertently caused. The guard listened with a mixture of impatience and understanding and was about to issue a warning when his wireless phone crackled to life.

The voice of the loco pilot came through, sounding unusually tense. "There's something you need to know," he said, his tone laced with urgency. "The station master just contacted me. His linemen spotted suspicious men loitering near the tracks ahead. When approached, the men fled into the dark. Upon further inspection, the linemen found the tracks had been completely removed—about a quarter kilometre from our current position."

The guard's face turned ashen as he absorbed the news. The realization dawned on him that if the train had continued on its path, it would have sped straight into the missing section of track, leading to a derailment and untold disaster. He turned to Damu, his expression shifting from annoyance to a mixture of awe and gratitude.

"Your bag... pulling the chain may have just saved everyone on this train," he murmured, hardly able to believe it himself.

Lakshmi's eyes widened as the significance of the guard's words sank in. She looked at Damu, who appeared just as shocked, and then down at Vidya, grateful beyond words that her family and hundreds of other passengers had narrowly escaped tragedy. The guard quickly got to work, coordinating with the RPF and the station master to initiate repairs on the damaged track. Emergency crews were dispatched immediately, working tirelessly under the faint glow of dawn to replace the missing section of track.

Throughout the night, the passengers in Damu's compartment exchanged stories, theories, and feelings of gratitude. Most were unaware of the true gravity of the situation, but word of Damu's unintentional heroics gradually spread through the train. Some passengers even approached him to offer their thanks, their faces a mix of admiration and relief. Damu, though initially taken aback by the attention, graciously accepted their gratitude, his thoughts lingering on the uncanny turn of events.

By 8 a.m., the repairs were completed, and the train resumed its journey. The incident had delayed them by several hours, but there was a palpable sense of relief and camaraderie among the passengers, each of them quietly reflecting on how close they had come to disaster.

The rest of the journey passed without incident, and as the train finally pulled into Lucknow station later that evening, Damu, Lakshmi, and Vidya were greeted by Lakshmi's father and an unexpected crowd of curious onlookers. News of the incident had already spread, and several local reporters were waiting to interview the man whose accidental pull of the alarm chain had potentially saved hundreds of lives. Lakshmi's father looked on with pride, marvelling at the unexpected heroism of his son-in-law.

In the days that followed, the railway authorities sent Damu a formal letter of appreciation, acknowledging his inadvertent yet life-saving actions. The local media ran stories about the "unintentional saviour" whose misplaced luggage had averted tragedy. Although Damu was slightly embarrassed by all the attention, he couldn't deny the sense of pride he felt in having kept his family and fellow passengers safe.

Back in Kedarpur, friends and neighbours gathered around as Damu recounted the tale, from the journey's beginning at Dehradun station to the moment the train screeched to a halt. Each retelling brought fresh amazement and admiration, especially from the children, who regarded him as a true hero.

This story became a cherished family legend, retold at every gathering and celebration. For years, whenever someone in Kedarpur needed a reminder of the power of fate and the unexpected turns of life, they would recall Damu's journey to Lucknow. His tale became a symbol of courage and luck intertwined, proof that sometimes, even the smallest, most accidental acts can change the course of destiny.

And for Damu, each glance at the luggage bag that had once dangled from the emergency chain served as a gentle reminder of that unforgettable journey—a journey where a hanging bag, a sharp jolt, and the alarm chain had come together in a fateful harmony, saving lives and turning an ordinary man into an unlikely hero.

EPISODE - 7

"Damu's Flask of Justice"

The end of the year arrived with a celebratory atmosphere in Kedarpur, a quaint but vibrant town. Though small, it had a unique charm, nestled among the hills near Dehradun. The town thrived with excitement as people shopped for Christmas and New Year's festivities, eager to end the year on a joyful note. Bright lights adorned storefronts, and colourful banners flapped above the bustling streets. Like many towns across India, Kedarpur came alive with holiday cheer. The festive week, starting with Christmas Eve and stretching through to New Year's Day, was a time when people shopped, met friends, and celebrated with loved ones.

But amid the joy, a dark shadow loomed over Dehradun and neighbouring towns, as an elusive chain-snatching gang terrorized the area. Operating with a relentless and professional approach, the gang preyed on unsuspecting women, particularly senior citizens out for morning walks, ladies decorating the fronts of their houses with rangoli, and even children on their way to school. The gang's modus operandi was precise: two men, both helmeted and riding a motorbike, would pull up, snatch a gold chain, and disappear before their victim had a chance to react. The gang had become notorious for skillfully avoiding CCTV cameras, staying one step ahead of the police.

In Dehradun, Police Inspector Ranjith was particularly troubled by the crime wave. Despite the best efforts of his team, the gang remained a step ahead, taunting the police with their elusive nature. The chain snatchers had evaded capture so well that frustration simmered at police headquarters. Commissioner Mithun Sharma called Ranjith in for a high-level meeting to discuss the case, his tone serious but encouraging. Commissioner Sharma knew Ranjith's potential and had seen him solve high-profile cases in the past. With the help of his old friend Damu, Ranjith had previously cracked cases involving a market bomb threat, a child kidnapping ring, a highway heist, and an ATM robbery. Each time, Damu had proven to be an invaluable ally, his quick wit and unconventional methods making him a local hero.

As the New Year dawned, Ranjith redoubled his commitment to finding the chain snatchers. Back in Kedarpur, the morning of January 1st broke with a chill in the air. Damu, with his usual enthusiasm, decided to begin his New Year with a walk to the nearby park, carrying a steel flask filled with hot water, which he slung around his neck. Meanwhile, his wife Lakshmi and daughter Vidya were absorbed in the vibrant patterns of a rangoli they were crafting outside their house. The rangoli's bright colours contrasted beautifully against the grey of the street, and neighbours stopped to admire their handiwork.

At the park, Damu greeted friends and exchanged New Year's wishes, his warm, friendly personality drawing others to him. As he began his walk home, he spotted a familiar face—Inderjit Singh, an old family friend and one of his father's former students. Damu's father, Jitendhar, had been a beloved teacher, and his house was once a gathering place for many of his students. Over the years, many of them rose to prominent positions in various fields, from government to the police force. Ranjith was one of these students, while Inderjit had become a successful gym owner in Kedarpur. Known for his muscular build and intimidating appearance, Inderjit was a gentle giant at heart, a loyal friend to those he cared about.

"Happy New Year, Inderjit!" Damu greeted him with a hearty handshake. They exchanged a few nostalgic stories, reminiscing about Damu's father and the impact he'd had on so many lives. Damu invited Inderjit over for tea, eager to introduce him to Lakshmi and Vidya.

As they approached Damu's home, they saw Lakshmi and Vidya carefully applying the final touches to the rangoli. Its colours spread like a burst of joy on the ground, adding a festive spirit to the already celebratory day. Just then, a motorcycle sped down the street and screeched to a halt near the house, causing Damu and Inderjit to glance over with mild curiosity. The rider and the pillion, both wearing helmets, appeared to be lost. The pillion rider held out a slip of paper, gesturing for Vidya to take it, as if asking for directions. The interaction seemed innocent at first, but Lakshmi's instincts sensed something was amiss.

In a split second, the pillion rider lunged forward, his hand reaching for the gold chain around Lakshmi's neck. Reacting swiftly, Lakshmi grabbed a cup of color powder and flung it at him, the vibrant powder exploding onto the driver's face, blinding him momentarily. Inderjit sprang into action, his imposing frame a deterrent, but the snatcher still tried to flee.

The blinded driver panicked, revving the engine as he attempted to escape. But fate intervened in an unexpected way. Damu's steel flask, which he'd been carrying casually, slipped from his hands and rolled into the street, coming to rest directly in the motorcycle's path. The bike's front wheel hit the flask, causing the vehicle to skid violently. The pillion rider was thrown off, landing near Inderjit, who wasted no time in restraining him. Meanwhile, the driver struggled to free himself from the fallen bike, his leg pinned awkwardly beneath it.

Inderjit, with impressive strength, hauled the injured driver upright, while still holding the pillion in a vice-like grip. Damu quickly called Ranjith, who was already on high alert. He explained the situation, urging him to come to the house immediately.

Within minutes, Ranjith and his team arrived, sirens piercing the quiet of the New Year's morning. He took one look at the two captives and realized these were the men he'd been after for weeks. Under Ranjith's stern interrogation at the police station, the gang members eventually confessed, detailing their entire network and revealing the hideouts of their associates. Ranjith's eyes sparkled with satisfaction as he updated Commissioner Mithun Sharma, who expressed his admiration for Ranjith's persistence and praised Damu's unintentional but brilliant assistance.

Thanks to Damu's unwitting intervention and Lakshmi's quick thinking, the entire chain-snatching gang was dismantled. The people of Dehradun and surrounding areas could finally breathe a sigh of relief, knowing the streets were safer.

As evening settled over Kedarpur, a quiet joy filled Damu's home. The family had prepared sweets, their dining table adorned with an array of festive treats—laddoos, jalebis, and barfis, gleaming like jewels in the soft light. Damu, Ranjith, and Inderjit gathered around, sharing stories of the day's events and exchanging laughter. Vidya recounted her surprise at the unexpected drama, while Lakshmi's eyes shone with pride.

"To a safe and prosperous New Year," Damu toasted, raising his glass of warm chai. Ranjith and Inderjit clinked their cups with his, their laughter filling the room.

At that moment, they savoured more than just sweets—they savoured friendship, family, and the triumph of justice, all made possible by the most unexpected of heroes: a rolling steel flask and a brave-hearted family.

EPISODE - 8

"The Misstep that saved the Bank"

It was a quiet afternoon in Kedarpur when Damu, found himself on an errand with his friend Ranjith, Inspector of Police, Ranjith's and Damu's common friend Inderjith. The three friends planned to stop by the bank so Damu could withdraw money for an upcoming festival. Ranjith, ever vigilant, had opted to dress casually, his plain clothes disguising his true identity.

They arrived at the bank, exchanging pleasantries with a few of the staff before settling in to wait. The bank was small, one of those places where everyone knew each other, and Damu felt at ease. Little did he know that three masked men were watching from outside, preparing to strike.

In the blink of an eye, the robbers burst into the bank, shouting commands as they locked the doors behind them. One robber, tall and wiry, aimed his gun skyward and fired a warning shot, sending everyone to the floor in a panic. "Nobody moves! Hand over your phones," he ordered.

Damu, frightened and bewildered, fumbled with his phone. Ranjith gave him a reassuring nod, signalling him to comply and stay calm. One of the robbers went around collecting phones from the terrified staff and customers, including Damu, Ranjith, and Inderjith. They didn't realize they had rounded up an officer and his sharp-minded colleague among their hostages.

The robbers quickly assessed their situation. One of them, a burly man with a scar running down his cheek, scanned the room. His gaze settled on Damu, his expression changing slightly, a flicker of recognition in his eyes. He whispered to the leader, "Boss, that guy looks like the one from the news. The one who helped catch those smugglers."

The leader, a stout man with a gruff voice, looked at Damu with suspicion, unsure what to make of the nervous-looking fellow. The robber's hesitation intensified as he recalled the news report, which had hailed Damu's unintentional heroics after his accidental capture of a notorious gang. Though Damu had stumbled into that situation entirely by chance, the news report had framed him as a vigilante of sorts.

"Take him as a hostage. If he's a big shot, it'll get the cops off our back," the leader barked, shoving Damu toward the centre of the room. Damu's wide-eyed innocence and frantic stammering didn't ease their suspicion. The leader ordered Damu to turn around, intending to restrain him tightly.

As Damu nervously complied, he backed up, his foot hitting the corner of a welcome mat. In his haste, he stepped on it awkwardly, and before he knew it, he slipped, flailing backwards as he lost his balance. In a moment of sheer, unintended luck, Damu toppled into the leader, who staggered back, completely caught off guard. The impact sent the leader sprawling, his gun flying out of his grip and skidding across the floor.

The entire room froze, eyes wide as Damu lay sprawled on the floor beside the astonished robber leader. The other two robbers were stunned by the sudden unexpected incident. Ranjith and Inderjith exchanged a quick look, recognizing the opportunity.

Seizing the moment, Ranjith sprang to his feet and tackled the robber nearest to him. Inderjith, displaying lightning reflexes, grabbed a metal paperweight from a nearby counter and threw it at the third robber's hand, disarming him. The crowd gasped, watching as the plainclothes policemen subdued the robbers with remarkable precision and control.

Meanwhile, Damu scrambled to his feet, dusting himself off, still bewildered by the chaos unfolding around him. His accidental fall had not only disarmed the leader but had also created the distraction Ranjith and Inderjith needed to neutralize the threat.

Within minutes, Ranjith and Inderjith had the robbers on the ground, hands restrained behind their backs. Ranjith immediately collected his mobile and dialled his station and called for patrol. The bank manager, realizing the ordeal was over, rushed to unlock the doors and let the police in. The officers who arrived on the scene were quick to assist, securing the three robbers in handcuffs and escorting them outside as a crowd began to gather, eager to see the unexpected hero of the day.

Damu, still reeling from the unplanned adventure, tried to wrap his head around what had just happened. He felt a strange mix of embarrassment and relief, glancing over at Ranjith, who couldn't help but chuckle at his friend's flustered expression.

"Damu, you've done it again," Ranjith said, clapping him on the shoulder. "You really have a knack for this!"

"But—I didn't do anything! I just slipped," Damu protested, his cheeks flushing.

"That's the beauty of it," Inderjith added with a grin. "Your unintentional heroics are your charm. We couldn't have planned that better ourselves!"

The staff and customers gathered around, many of them thanking Damu for his "bravery," much to his dismay. He tried to explain that it was all an accident, but his explanations only seemed to add to the legend growing around him.

News of the foiled robbery spread through Kedarpur like wildfire, with Damu once again finding himself the subject of attention. Reporters came to interview him, showering him with praise for his "selfless act of courage," while Damu, thoroughly embarrassed, insisted that he was just an ordinary man with no intentions of heroism. He repeated time and again that he had simply slipped on a mat, but no one seemed to listen.

Back at home, Damu's wife Lakshmi and their daughter Vidya were both proud and amused by the entire affair. Lakshmi, always aware of her husband's innocent nature, couldn't help but laugh. "You've really become the talk of the town, Damu," she teased. "Just be careful where you walk next time!"

Damu sighed, grateful that the ordeal was over but still baffled by the attention. He looked at Ranjith, who had stayed to have tea with the family, and muttered, "One of these days, I'd like to go somewhere without ending up in the newspaper."

Ranjith grinned. "Damu, you've got a gift. Not everyone can pull off what you do by accident. Just think of it as fate looking out for you."

Damu chuckled, finally giving in to the humour of the situation. Though he never sought the spotlight, he couldn't deny that these unintended moments of heroism had brought him closer to his friends and family. And who knows? Maybe his unintentional slip-ups were meant to guide him to protect those around him in ways he'd never understand.

As the sun set over Kedarpur, Damu found himself grateful—not for the attention, but for the friends who had his back and the family who believed in him. In his heart, he knew he'd always be the same simple man. But perhaps, just perhaps, he'd grown a little braver along the way, even if by accident.

****

Disclaimer

This book is a work of fiction. Names, characters, places, and incidents either are the product of the author's imagination or are used fictitiously. Any resemblance to actual persons, living or dead, events, or locales is entirely coincidental.

The story is set in an Indian town and is intended for children aged 8 years and above. While inspired by cultural elements and settings, it does not represent any specific town, community, or cultural practice.

Readers are encouraged to enjoy the story as a creative work of fiction and not as a reflection of real events or individuals.